Peace And Love

Blank Sketchbook

100 blank pages

THIS BOOK BELONGS TO:

____